Lord Jesus,

you invite us to take up our cross each day
in our following of you.

But today, it is your Cross and your Way that we follow.
Give us courage and perseverance in this journey of love
that we make with you. In our weakness, you give us
strength, in that strength, help us always to be faithful to
you, our Lord and Master.

Jesus is judged and condemned

"He was a man of sorrows, familiar with suffering."
(Isaiah 53.3)

First Station

Jesus was used to being judged and very often that judgement was made in ignorance.

He was accustomed to being the prophet who was not accepted in his own country.

But the judgement we are witnessing now is altogether different.
This is a judgement for death – and for what?
He is being condemned because he brought Good News to the afflicted, sight to the blind, liberty to captives, freedom for the oppressed. He dared to proclaim and embody the love and mercy of God.

His sorrow and sadness are for us because we are unable to recognize his love and our own need of it.
His suffering is physical but, even more acutely, spiritual because we are judging him. When we do this and when we condemn him, we turn our backs on the light of his love. We choose to walk in the dark.

Jesus, have mercy and forgive us.

I love you, Jesus, my love, above all things;
I repent with my whole heart for having offended you.
Never permit me to separate myself from you again.
Grant that I may love you always;
and then do with me what you will.

Jesus receives the Cross

"Ours were the sufferings he bore; ours the sorrows he carried."
(Isaiah 53.4)

Second Station

This man before our eyes is the Jesus who shed tears over Jerusalem and he sheds tears over us. But he does not condemn. He only hopes that by his taking our weaknesses and failures on his shoulders, somehow we will be able to find the yoke easier and the burden lighter.

As the Cross is laid on him, he lifts our sufferings and our sorrows from our shoulders on to his. His heart rejoices because he knows he is finding the ones who are lost. He now can bring us to his Father and there will be great rejoicing in heaven.

Jesus, have mercy and forgive us.

I love you, Jesus, my love, above all things;
I repent with my whole heart for having offended you.
Never permit me to separate myself from you again.
Grant that I may love you always;
and then do with me what you will.

Jesus falls for the first time

"We thought of him as someone punished, struck by God and brought low."
(Isaiah 53.4)

Third Station

Sad processions through the busy narrow streets of Jerusalem like this one were a familiar sight for the bystanders. They would have scarcely given it a second thought.

But this was different because there were disciples and followers in the crowd. A few hours ago they had run away; they had denied that they had ever known him.

As they watched him now, they knew, deep in their hearts, that he was not just stumbling and falling from weakness, he was suffering because his heart had been broken by betrayal and fear. He had given everything and, as he saw his gift rejected, he was overwhelmed. He stumbled and fell.

Jesus, have mercy and forgive us.

I love you, Jesus, my love, above all things;
I repent with my whole heart for having offended you.
Never permit me to separate myself from you again.
Grant that I may love you always;
and then do with me what you will.

Jesus is met by his mother

"Like a sapling, he grew up in front of us; like a root in arid ground."
(Isaiah 53.2)

Fourth Station

Mary had been with Jesus from the first moment of his conception. She had seen him grow like a sapling in the arid ground of poverty and obscurity in Nazareth.

She had pondered all that had been said about him and she had listened to his words. She had witnessed his miracles and had listened to his teaching. She had come to that fullness of faith, which is a love beyond all understanding.

But she knew too that a sword would pierce her heart, as it was to pierce his. This was that moment and she was helpless. She could only suffer with him whom she now saw so cruelly treated.

As she suffered with him, so she suffers with us and for us because we are the Church; we are the Body of Christ.

Jesus, have mercy and forgive us.

I love you, Jesus, my love, above all things;
I repent with my whole heart for having offended you.
Never permit me to separate myself from you again.
Grant that I may love you always;
and then do with me what you will.

Simon of Cyrene carries the Cross

"By force and by law he was taken; would anyone plead his cause?"
(Isaiah 53.8)

Fifth Station

Without a doubt, his disciples were heart-broken at what they saw as they lurked, facelessly, at the back of the crowd. Nevertheless, none of them came forward to help.

In the end, it was Simon of Cyrene who was constrained to help Jesus. Reluctant he may have been, but surely he was graced for the task and privilege that was thrust upon him. He had probably never heard Jesus inviting the weary and the overburdened to come to him and yet it was now the same Lord who came to Simon and invited him to carry his Cross.

As they saw this stranger helping their Lord and Master, the disciples can only have felt more and more ashamed and miserable.

Jesus, have mercy and forgive us.

I love you, Jesus, my love, above all things;
I repent with my whole heart for having offended you.
Never permit me to separate myself from you again.
Grant that I may love you always;
and then do with me what you will.

Veronica wipes the face of Jesus

"A man to make people screen their faces, he was despised and we took no account of him." *(Isaiah 53.3)*

Sixth Station

Isaiah's words had no resonance for Veronica; this was not the way she saw it.

We know nothing of her except the legend that gives us this station. But in our hearts we know it must be true. Among those closest to Jesus were many women and many of them had been forgiven their sins and cured of the evils that afflicted them.

Perhaps Veronica was one of these. Perhaps she had looked at the face of Jesus and into his eyes and there had seen unimaginable love and compassion. She could not now turn away from the face that had brought her back to life and into love. She had to show compassion and tenderness to the one who had shown her so much love. She wiped his face and her gesture of love has never been forgotten.

Jesus, have mercy and forgive us.

I love you, Jesus, my love, above all things;
I repent with my whole heart for having offended you.
Never permit me to separate myself from you again.
Grant that I may love you always;
and then do with me what you will.

Jesus falls the second time

"He was crushed for our sins."
(Isaiah 53.5)

Seventh Station

There can be nothing worse or more hurtful than being let down and betrayed by one who is a friend. Jesus had experienced that rejection and now the thought of it forces him to his knees.

He had invested so much of himself in the friendship and love he had for his disciples. He had cared for them, loved them, taught them and had been their intimate friend. He had not called them servants but friends and had shared with them the deepest secrets of his life.

Their betrayal – and the very thought of it – now caused his knees to buckle so that he falls. Not even the stalwart help of Simon was able to help him.

And yet he rises again; he forgives and he staggers on because "it is not yet accomplished".

Jesus, have mercy and forgive us.

I love you, Jesus, my love, above all things;
I repent with my whole heart for having offended you.
Never permit me to separate myself from you again.
Grant that I may love you always;
and then do with me what you will.

Jesus speaks to the women of Jerusalem

"He let himself be taken for a sinner while he was bearing the faults of many and praying all the time for sinners." *(Isaiah 53.12)*

Eighth Station

Only the greatest and the best among us can set aside our own sufferings and sorrows when we meet with the distress and anguish of others.

The women of Jerusalem were surely compassionate women and were appalled by what they saw being done to one who they knew was a good man. After all, had he not sat with them and talked with them in the courtyards of the Temple?

But now he was more concerned for them. He does not just accept their compassion, he comforts them and challenges them by his firm words of tenderness and love.

Even in moments of impenetrable darkness, this is the one who is the light of the world. Whoever follows him and listens to him will never walk in the dark but will have the light of life.

Jesus, have mercy and forgive us.

I love you, Jesus, my love, above all things;
I repent with my whole heart for having offended you.
Never permit me to separate myself from you again.
Grant that I may love you always;
and then do with me what you will.

Jesus falls the third time

"The Lord has been pleased to crush him with suffering."
(Isaiah 53.10)

Ninth Station

Peter once asked Jesus a very reasonable question: "How often must I forgive someone who wrongs me?" Jesus' answer is very simple and quite uncompromising. "Always," he says.

When fall after fall and sin after sin are such a feature of our lives, it is wonderful to be able to know – with confidence and absolute trust – that we can come again and again to Jesus for healing and forgiveness.

His determination to rise again after yet another fall, crushed as he was by suffering and fear, gives him the authority, the power and the love to forgive us whenever we turn to him. Because of his courage and his steadfastness on this way of the Cross, he has the absolute right to say to us that, as we go on our way, we must sin no more if we are to journey in the peace of his love.

Jesus, have mercy and forgive us.

I love you, Jesus, my love, above all things;
I repent with my whole heart for having offended you.
Never permit me to separate myself from you again.
Grant that I may love you always;
and then do with me what you will.

Jesus is stripped of his garments

"Harshly dealt with, he bore it humbly; he never opened his mouth."
(Isaiah 53.7)

Tenth Station

Public exposure is a most humiliating experience and when it happens, there is no hiding place.

Everything we are and all that we have done are paraded for all to see and people may make what judgements they like. Our fragile defences are destroyed and there is nothing we can say.

But there is another sort of exposure which is nothing as harsh. It is the look of love. This exposes us too but it brings warmth, acceptance and affirmation. The Scriptures often tell us that Jesus looked "steadily" at a person. When that happens – and it does happen to all of us – then our defences fall away and we find ourselves enfolded in his love which is at the heart of all loving. We should ask Peter because when he denied that he knew Jesus, the Lord turned and looked at him. We can be sure that look was one of intense love, mingled with sadness, but not condemnation. The experience reduced Peter to bitter tears then but he was to experience the utter joy of loving forgiveness when they met again at the lakeside in Galilee.

Jesus, have mercy and forgive us.

I love you, Jesus, my love, above all things;
I repent with my whole heart for having offended you.
Never permit me to separate myself from you again.
Grant that I may love you always;
and then do with me what you will.

Jesus is nailed to the Cross

"He was pierced through for our faults."
(Isaiah 53.5)

Eleventh Station

Those feet that had tramped the dusty roads and those hands that had always been open to bless, to comfort and to heal, had to be nailed to the Cross so that we should never forget the sweet pain of the Lord's love for us.

Arms outstretched, with hands nailed – these are the signs of the perpetual welcome that our redeeming Lord has for sinners.

But the journey into salvation is long and hard and there is no cheap grace – there are no shortcuts. We too are nailed to the Cross of Jesus in the circumstances of our lives and we can either resist this or accept it lovingly. When we freely accept it, we die and rise again with him to the life he has won for us, healed and forgiven.

Jesus, have mercy and forgive us.

I love you, Jesus, my love, above all things;
I repent with my whole heart for having offended you.
Never permit me to separate myself from you again.
Grant that I may love you always;
and then do with me what you will.

Jesus dies on the Cross

"He was torn away from the land of the living; for our faults, he was struck down in death." *(Isaiah 53.8)*

Twelfth Station

The sign of the Cross is one of the most instinctive and familiar gestures that we make.

Every time we so sign ourselves, we remember and give thanks that a priceless life has been laid down for us.

The remembering brings power. In this power we overcome sin and we are strengthened in our weaknesses – this is the triumph of the Cross.

For St Paul it is almost unthinkable that one person should die for another but, when it happens, it shows an unspeakable and almost unimaginable loving. "Greater love than this no one has than that life should be laid down for our friends."

Jesus says, "You are my friends, if you do what I command you." We are his friends and he has died for us and this, for us, is love, triumph and salvation.

Jesus, have mercy and forgive us.

I love you, Jesus, my love, above all things;
I repent with my whole heart for having offended you.
Never permit me to separate myself from you again.
Grant that I may love you always;
and then do with me what you will.

Jesus is taken down from the Cross

"His soul's anguish over, he shall see the light and be content."
(Isaiah 53.11)

Thirteenth Station

We last met Mary on the way to Calvary and now she is with us again.

Entrusted with the infant Church by Jesus as he died, named as mother of the Body of Christ, Mary now receives his broken, physical body into her arms with immense tenderness and reverence.

She has been closest to him in his suffering but now, through her tears and in the breaking of her heart, she begins to see that glorious light which is to burst on the world three days hence as he rises from the dead.

This is the body of Christ, her Son, of whom it was said that he was destined for the fall and rise of many in Israel – a sign of contradiction but the sign of life that contradicts and overcomes death. Mary, pray for us that we may have life, and have it to the full.

Jesus, have mercy and forgive us.

I love you, Jesus, my love, above all things;
I repent with my whole heart for having offended you.
Never permit me to separate myself from you again.
Grant that I may love you always;
and then do with me what you will.

Jesus is laid in the tomb

"They gave him a grave with the wicked, a tomb with the rich."
(Isaiah 53.9)

Fourteenth Station

The one who in life had nowhere to lay his head, a man noted for his poverty and simplicity, now finds himself buried with the rich and the privileged.

But it was a tomb that was only borrowed, for he would not lie there long. Early in the morning, on the third day, the tomb was empty when women came to anoint the body.

We must not stay by the empty tomb because he is not there. All that we can do now is to bury our sins, our failures and our weaknesses in the tomb where he lay. If our sinfulness is buried with Christ, that is where we leave it. Because he has risen, the new life of Easter now flows into our lives. We are transfigured and saved.

Jesus, have mercy and forgive us.

I love you, Jesus, my love, above all things;
I repent with my whole heart for having offended you.
Never permit me to separate myself from you again.
Grant that I may love you always;
and then do with me what you will.

Jesus is risen

"See, my servant will prosper, he shall be lifted up to great heights... the crowds will be astonished at him and kings will stand speechless before him." *(Isaiah 52.13,15)*

It took an unbeliever to proclaim Jesus as Son of God as he died on the Cross. It takes ordinary, sinful yet redeemed, men and women as we are to proclaim him Lord of Life now.

His anointing is our anointing, his dying is our dying, and his rising is our rising. In our Easter life, with him we now proclaim Good News to the afflicted, liberty to captives. With him, we bring new sight to the blind, freedom to the oppressed and the year of the Lord's favour.

Lord, now send us forth in your Spirit. Empower us to be your witnesses to the world so that all the ends of the earth may see the salvation of our God.

Jesus, have mercy and fill us with your love.

I love you, Jesus, my love, above all things;
I repent with my whole heart for having offended you.
Never permit me to separate myself from you again.
Grant that I may love you always;
and then do with me what you will.

Published by **Redemptorist Publications**

Copyright © 2004 Redemptorist Publications

Design: Peena Lad

ISBN 0 85231 298 9

Printed by Joseph Ball

Alphonsus House Chawton Hampshire GU34 3HQ
Telephone   01420 88222   Fax   01420 88805
rp@ShineOnline.net   www.ShineOnline.net